Raccoons

Victoria Blakemore

Copyright info/picture credits

Cover, Riverwalker/Adobestock; Page 3, klimkin/Pixabay; Page 5, naeimasgarys/Pixabay; Page 7, Alexas_Fotos/Pixabay; Page 9, GIS/Pixabay; Pages 10-11, Eléonore H/AdobeStock; Page 13, Vladimir Wrangel/AdobeStock; Page 15, jccain/AdobeStock; Page 17, Alexas_Fotos/Pixabay; Page 19, Digwin/Pixabay; Page 21, HealthyBacon/Pixabay; Page 23; tpsdave/Pixabay; Page 25, Riverwalker/Adobestock; Page 27, waldiwkl/Pixabay; Page 29, MonikaDesigns/Pixabay; Page 31, Cristopher Gonzalez/Flickr; Page 33, katka/Pixabay

Table of Contents

What Are Raccoons?

Raccoons are small mammals.

They are **nocturnal**, which

means they are most active at

night.

Raccoons are usually black,

gray, and white in color. Some

raccoons also have fur that is

red or brown in color.

Raccoons are known for the

black fur on their face. It can

look like a mask.

Size

Raccoons are usually the size of a small dog. They often weigh between fourteen and twenty-three pounds.

Male raccoons are larger than female raccoons.

Physical Characteristics

Raccoons usually have a long tail that is covered in black and gray stripes.

They have long fingers on their front paws. Their fingers can be used to grab and twist.

Raccoons also use their

fingers to grip when climbing.

Habitat

Raccoons are able to **adapt** to living in many different habitats. They are found in forests, marshes, prairies, mountains, and even cities.

Raccoons usually live near water.

Raccoons were first found in North America. They were brought to Europe in the 1930's.

Raccoons are now found in North America, Europe, and Asia.

Diet

Raccoons are **omnivores**, which means that they eat meat and plants.

Their diet is made up of crayfish, frogs, mice, bird eggs, fruit, and plants.

Raccoons can use their paws to

hold their food while they eat.

Raccoons do most of their hunting in and around the water. Many of their favorite foods are found by the water.

Although raccoons have food that they prefer, they will eat almost anything.

Raccoons can get into trash cans. They go through the garbage looking for food.

Communication

Raccoons use sound and smell to communicate with each other.

Scientists have found thirteen different calls made by raccoons. They are usually used between a mother and her babies.

Raccoons have a good sense of smell. They often use smell to find other raccoons.

Movement

Raccoons have been known to run at speeds of up to fifteen miles per hour.

They are also very good swimmers. Raccoons often swim to hunt for fish or to escape from predators.

Raccoons are very good

climbers.

Dens

Raccoons live in holes called dens. These dens are usually in hollow trees, logs, or burrows made by other animals.

In areas where people live, raccoon dens are sometimes found in attics or barns.

Raccoons usually make their
dens close to the water.

Raccoon Life

Some raccoons are **solitary**, which means that they spend their time alone.

Other raccoons live in family groups. A group of raccoons can be called a "nursery" or a "gaze."

Raccoon gazes have an easier

time hunting than raccoons

that are alone.

Raccoon Kits

Raccoons usually have a **litter** of up to 7 babies. Their babies are called kits.

When kits are first born, they are blind and have very fine hair. Their eyes will first open after two or three weeks.

Kits are usually born in the spring. They stay with their mother through the winter.

Do Raccoons Hibernate?

People used to think that raccoons **hibernate** in the winter.

This is not true. However, they often spend more time sleeping in their dens during the winter.

There is less food in the winter.

Raccoons sleep more to use

less energy.

Lifespan

In the wild, raccoons live between two and three years. In **captivity**, raccoons have lived up to twenty years.

The main threats facing raccoons are disease and **predators** like coyotes. Raccoons can also be hit by cars when crossing roads.

Population

The pygmy raccoon is **endangered**. It is only found on Cozumel Island in Mexico.

All other raccoon species are not endangered. Their populations have been growing.

In 2016, there were fewer than 1,000 pygmy raccoons in the wild.

Feeding Raccoons

Some people like to feed raccoons because they are cute. If people feed them, they will get used to coming up to people.

Raccoons are wild animals. They can be **aggressive** or they could be sick.

Raccoons are wild animals.

They should be left alone.

Glossary

Adapt: to change, adjust

Aggressive: mean, likely to attack

Captivity: animals that are kept

by humans, not in the wild

Endangered: at risk of becoming

extinct

Hibernate: to sleep through the

winter to save energy

Litter: a group of young animals born at one time

Nocturnal: animals that are active at night and sleep during the day

Omnivores: an animal that eats plants and animals

Predator: an animal that hunts other animals

Solitary: living alone

About the Author

Victoria Blakemore is a first grade

teacher in Southwest Florida with a

passion for reading.

You can visit her at

www.elementaryexplorers.com

Also in This Series

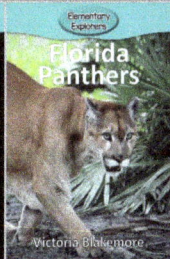

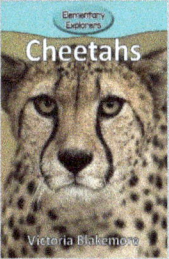

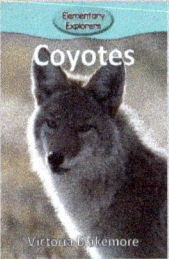

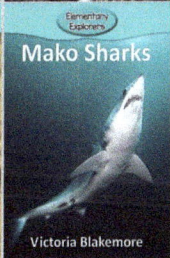

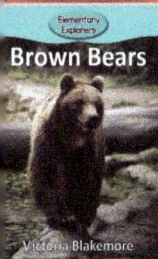

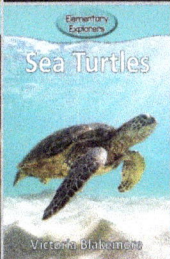

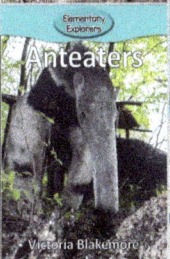

Chameleons — Victoria Blakemore
Florida Panthers — Victoria Blakemore
Aye-Ayes — Victoria Blakemore
Black Bears — Victoria Blakemore
Cheetahs — Victoria Blakemore
Manatees — Victoria Blakemore

Gingerbread — Victoria Blakemore
Polar Bears — Victoria Blakemore
Hot Chocolate — Victoria Blakemore
Orangutans — Victoria Blakemore
Coyotes — Victoria Blakemore
Marshmallows — Victoria Blakemore

Strawberries — Victoria Blakemore
Aardvarks — Victoria Blakemore
Mako Sharks — Victoria Blakemore
Alligators — Victoria Blakemore
Frogs — Victoria Blakemore
Hedgehogs — Victoria Blakemore

Brown Bears — Victoria Blakemore
Bongos — Victoria Blakemore
Sea Turtles — Victoria Blakemore
Quokkas — Victoria Blakemore
Muskrats — Victoria Blakemore
Zebras — Victoria Blakemore

Red Foxes — Victoria Blakemore
Ring-Tailed Lemurs — Victoria Blakemore
Platypuses — Victoria Blakemore
Anteaters — Victoria Blakemore
Kangaroos — Victoria Blakemore
Rhinos — Victoria Blakemore

Jaguars — Victoria Blakemore
Wombats — Victoria Blakemore

Elementary Explorers

Also in This Series

Chameleons	Florida Panthers	Aye-Ayes	Black Bears	Cheetahs	Manatees
Gingerbread	Polar Bears	Hot Chocolate	Orangutans	Coyotes	Marshmallows
Strawberries	Aardvarks	Mako Sharks	Alligators	Frogs	Hedgehogs
Brown Bears	Bongos	Sea Turtles	Quokkas	Muskrats	Zebras
Red Foxes	Ring-Tailed Lemurs	Platypuses	Anteaters	Kangaroos	Rhinos
Jaguars	Wombats				

Elementary Explorers

Victoria Blakemore